School, Why Am I Here?

Unraveling the mystery of education and strengthening America's future

History, Language Arts, Art, Math, Science, and Sports

Zenith Publishing–USA

School, Why Am I Here? Unraveling the mysteries of an education and strengthening America's future. Copyright © 2011 by Zenith Publishing. Proudly printed and bound in the United States of America. All rights reserved. No part of this book shall be reproduced or transmitted in any form or by any means without permission in writing from the publisher. All requests, comments, or concerns should be sent to:

Zenith Publishing
P.O. Box 6371
Aurora, IL 60598-6371

Visit our web site at www.understandingschool.com for additional information.

Although the publisher has made every effort to ensure the accuracy and completeness of the information contained in the book, no liability for errors, omissions, or inconsistency shall be assumed. All information is believed to be accurate upon print.

LCCN 2011935390

ISBN 0-976-44282-5

Illustrations by Gary Young
Edited by Pentouch Communications
Cover by Borel Graphics

Dedication

This book is dedicated to my son. May you leverage your talents to reach your zenith!

Acknowledgements

I give thanks to God for blessing me with many talents and giving me the courage to accomplish my goals. Thank you to my wife for her love and support. Thank you to my parents for doing an outstanding job of raising me. Thanks to Pastor Jackson for continually challenging us to be productive and make a positive impact.

Special thanks to all of my teachers along the way who helped mold me into a productive person.

Contents

Introduction	1

<u>Covered Topics</u>:

History	**19**
Language Arts	**24**
Art	**32**
Math	**35**
Science	**40**
Sports	**47**
Conclusions	**53**
About the Author	**57**
About the Illustrator	**58**

Introduction

School. Some hate it; others love it. Most people go through the entire educational process without gaining a full understanding of why school is so important.

Indeed, a strong connection exists between getting good grades in school and "making something of your life." Yet, I believe this simple analogy is no longer sufficient to motivate a young person like you toward academic success.

This book was born out of a question I asked myself in tenth grade concerning why the subject matters I was studying in school were important. I vowed at that point to one day answer the question of whether reading Shakespearean plays, solving complex math equations, analyzing history (old news), and getting good grades really mattered in "the real world." Nearly 15 years later, as I approached my 30th birthday, I was reminded of this question, and the following is my conclusion and gift to you on why learning the "stuff" you study in school has true value.

Education as a Choice

Unfortunately, in this country a formal education is a requirement. I chose the word "unfortunately" to signify that when something is mandatory, people usually fail to appreciate the intent of the mandate.

As I hope you will discover through reading this material, education does play an important role in your overall success story. Although learning can be fun, education was never meant to compete with hanging out with your friends, surfing the Internet, playing ball, or watching television. The average person would prefer talking with friends over doing homework, watching television over being in school, and enjoying a night out on the town over studying for an exam.

If you would naturally prefer these activities over school-related tasks, I would classify you as normal. However, I've learned over time, that to be successful you must sometimes put off having fun to take care of more important things in life.

Key Principle: Education is a very important area of your life, and you must learn to voluntarily choose it over other available activities if you want to succeed.

The Purpose of School

The stated purposes of education have evolved and have been hotly debated throughout t American history as the needs of our maturing country changed over time. The Puritans felt that learning how to read was the practical end result of an education because it equipped youth with the ability to read the Bible. Fast-forwarding to the early 20th century, the business community felt that education should be more tailored to equip students with vocational skills. Today, educational goals seem to center around a need to stay competitive in a global marketplace.

Regardless of a particular point in time, the chief overall national purpose of formalized schooling is to secure a viable future for a given society. This is why the subtitle of this book includes the phrase "strengthening America's future." Today our educational system provides a means for developing individuals' talents into consumable resources and transfers nationalistic ideals—"American values"—into the hearts and minds of young people.

In a capitalistic society, the end product of a national education system is to establish a skilled workforce wherein individuals exchange developed skills or "know-how" for a given price or wage. The exchange of money for know-how, along with adherence to just laws, helps to establish a viable economy, which monetarily sustains the citizens of our country. In return, an abundance of available know-how and an ability/willingness to pay for such know-how leads to growth within our economic system.

This concept brings us to your primary purpose of going to school, which is to train you into a productive person. Webster defines the term "productive" simply as:

1.   The act of producing;

2.   Producing abundantly.

| Key Principle: You are in school to learn how to be a producer, which translates into being a person who adds tangible value to the world around you. |

Here is an example of how individuals can add tangible value:

"Jennifer" graduates from college with a developed skill. She applies for and accepts a job offer from a company seeking a college graduate with her particular skill set. The newly hired employee receives a starting salary of $50,000 to help the company reach its goals. Jennifer now has money to support herself and funnels money back into the economy through purchasing goods and services. Leveraging her experience and business relationships over time, she takes her savings and starts her own business. In effect, she evolves from being a student seeking knowledge to an employer who provides products/services globally and financially supports her employees and the community at large through employment opportunities, local tax payments, and corporate donations.

The Case Against Dropping Out

"Jessica" gets expelled out of her high school for fighting. She never liked school in the first place and decides to officially drop out. Her decision to not return to school doesn't sit well with her mom, and after multiple arguments Jessica decides it's best for her to move in with her older boyfriend, "Tony." She gets a job at a fast-food restaurant, but despite working double shifts her paychecks seem to be pretty small. She sees a television commercial about joining the military and thinks that the armed services might not be a bad career choice until a recruiter informs her that she must be a high school graduate to enlist. She looks for job opportunities online, but they all require a high school diploma and some college coursework as well. Tony tells her not to worry because he knows how to make money. Months later, Jessica discovers she is pregnant around the same time that Tony gets busted for drug trafficking. The following year Jessica finds herself raising a baby alone while Tony is locked up for a minimum 10-year sentence. After reviewing her limited options, she determines that public assistance is required to meet her and her baby's basic needs. Looking back at the poor life decisions she has made makes Jessica depressed and frustrated. Consequently, she becomes dependent on drugs and alcohol just to make it through each day.

Contrasting the two example illustrations should help simplify why dropping out of school, especially before graduating from high school, is such a bad idea. A person who foolishly drops out of school typically enters the job market without a fully developed skill.

Without developed know-how, the undereducated have a difficult time finding an employer who will pay them a livable wage to support themselves or investors to finance their entrepreneurial ideas.

Education attainment becomes a legal discriminatory barrier that prevents them from securing legal high wages. Compounding the problem, due largely to globalization, high-wage entry-level factory jobs are no longer a viable option for young people entering the American workforce. As a result, the undereducated end up working two or three low-wage jobs just to pay the bills. When you add children into this scenario, the individual's ability to secure and maintain a decent standard of living becomes extremely difficult. The heavy burden of trying to stay afloat can often lead to low-income public assistance, criminal activity, and/or drug abuse, which is often repeated by their children as well.

Therefore, instead of supporting families and the community at large, the undereducated may end up needing public support just to sustain the basics of food, clothing, and shelter, which drains resources out of the American economy.

This is why improving our school systems has gained so much interest in recent years. Your potential as an educated person is great. However, if you fail to maximize your educational opportunity, you, as an individual, and our society, as a whole, will not reap the benefits of adding additional producers into our economic system. This damaging turn of events in aggregate will also negatively contribute to the loss of the United States' competitive edge around the world.

The End Means to an Education is Not a Job

The United States has enjoyed a strong economic environment throughout most of its history. Premium employment opportunities have been available to those who are educated. Based on these facts, the notion of "go to college and get a good job" has held true over at least the last half century.

Today, going to college and receiving a degree no longer guarantees that you will be able to find a desirable job and obtain financial security. Unfortunately, under the current economic landscape, many recent college grads are settling for minimum wage work or moving back in with their parents. Is all hope lost?

No. The evolving global economy now requires you to focus on why you are in school in the first place. Importantly, you are not in school to ultimately get a job. On the contrary, as previously discussed, you are in school to master the skill of being productive.

As a consequence, if no employers are hiring, then you must find a different avenue to bring value to the market. For example, you could take your know-how and start your own business which could include simply doing contracted free lance work or formally establishing your own corporation.

Consider the following information regarding a few of American's youngest billionaires:

- Mark Zuckerberg, founder of Facebook, age 27, estimated net worth $6.9 billion.

- Andrew Mason, creator of Groupon, age 30, estimated net worth $1 billion.

- Sergey Brin and Larry Page, co-founders of Google, age 38, estimated combined net worth $40 billion.

These young company founders were focused on bringing something new to the market rather than simply trying to find a job. Their estimated fortunes prove that the sky is the limit if you adopt the right mindset about the opportunities you have available to you as an American.

> **Key Principle: The end result of your formal education is not a job. Your education is an important survival toolkit that will help you produce various sources of income, regardless of a particular economic environment.**

Understanding What's Behind School Structure

School is structured to mimic the real world or what I will term moving forward as the "marketplace." As a result, this is why there is a strong connection between doing well in school and succeeding in adult life.

> **Key Principle: School is a practice run for what you will face as an adult; the sooner you understand and master this concept the better off you will be later in life.**

School Attendance

When I was in school I was fortunate enough to be in good health, so I rarely missed many days. I remember receiving numerous perfect attendance awards, and although I appreciated the recognition, the achievement never meant that much to me.

You may believe that missing a few days of school occasionally is no big deal, but is this line of thinking correct? The answer lies within school's overall mission of helping you to become a productive person.

Isn't it difficult to fully grasp class assignments when you miss school? While you are at home, your classmates are taking advantage of hearing the teacher's firsthand presentation of the information being conveyed and they are able to ask questions along the way. When you return from your absence, not only has the class moved on to new material, but you also receive, at best, a condensed version of the information you missed. A steady pattern of receiving condensed information will cause you to fall behind your classmates, which will result in you acquiring less knowledge on the subject matters than they do.

As a further illustration, did you know that the government has placed an attendance mandate on your particular public school district? It is written law that school districts that fail to achieve a certain student attendance percentage aren't eligible to receive governmental funds. This is why some districts around the country had resorted in the past to raffling off free cars to students who had perfect attendance as a means of boosting their attendance scores above set standards.

Beyond the enticement of government dollars and a chance to win a car, this mandate illustrates a powerful concept that you as a student must understand.

> **Key Principle: The only way that you can effectively learn is to be consistently present.**

You can only be productive if you are present. From a real world application, you are only going to develop your talents into skills if you consistently come to school. Fact, attendance is directly tied to performance. Consider the following example:

You own Company X, and you have an employee who frequently calls off from work for various reasons. While he is away from work, he misses numerous meetings. Unnecessary time is spent trying to bring him up to speed when he returns. Your managers tend to skim over details they previously covered, so the employee occasionally makes critical mistakes in his assigned job responsibilities.

What would be your overall opinion of this employee? You answered honestly if you said that this employee would be the first one laid off or terminated when necessary. Why would you let him go? Your answer should essentially be that people with poor attendance records do not fare well in the marketplace because of their inability to produce.

Remember, you can't be productive at home lying on the couch when someone is paying you to complete certain tasks.

Therefore, I strongly caution you against simply not going to school when you don't feel like it. You may say it's raining too hard; I'm not going to school. It's too cold; I'm not going to school. I stayed up too late last night and didn't get enough rest; I'm not going to school. This attitude stifles your education and sets you up to be a fair weather worker characterized as undependable and non-productive. In turn, you will not be able to hold long-term employment or your entrepreneurial pursuits will be unsuccessful, which will affect your ability to accumulate wealth.

Grades

One of the biggest mistakes to come out of modern-day psychology is the notion that everybody is a winner no matter how well they perform. If this school of thought were true, then determine whether the following two statements would be considered acceptable:

1. The United States is just an average country instead of being a world leader. Acceptable?

2. It doesn't matter if your favorite sports team ever wins any games or becomes a league champion as long as they have fun playing together. Acceptable?

In your analysis, I hope you disagreed with both of these statements.

1. As Americans, we would prefer to be a world leader rather than merely citizens of an average country.

2. Part of the fun of following any sports team is cheering them on to win the coveted championship trophy at the end of the season.

In school, grades are a form of competition. In fact, the desire to receive the highest grade on a test helped drive me to academic success. If you look at grades as a form of competition, then it is difficult to understand how some top "competitive" athletes perform so poorly in school. Similar to the playing field, grades are a student's scorecard.

What is the importance of receiving a grade in the first place? The answer is that grades are a measurement of how effectively you are building your know-how. Receiving an A in a particular class demonstrates that you have a firm understanding of the subject matter and, more importantly, demonstrates that you can be counted on to apply the information when needed. Receiving a C in a class demonstrates that you have some understanding of the subject matter; yet, there is a high probability that you may, at times, struggle to apply the information when needed. Receiving a D or a F in a class subject demonstrates that you have little to no understanding of the information presented and it would be unreasonable to rely on you to apply the given information. Once again, you should start to see the real world application of why you receive grades. In the marketplace, you will be presenting your skills in exchange for money. A track record of poor grades gives consumers of your skills (employers, investors, and businesses/individuals) little confidence that you will be able to complete their required tasks in a timely professional manner. On the other hand, a track record of good grades demonstrates that you have the know-how to be both efficient and productive. This confidence in what you can deliver typically equals higher earnings, signing bonuses, and greater financial security during economic downturns. This is why job applications ask for your high school and college grade point averages. The greater abundance of skilled labor (ideally those with good grades), the more selective consumers can be when paying for individuals' skills.

To further illustrate this concept, what happens when you move from your current grade to the next grade up? Your report card typically says you have been "Promoted." How did you get this promotion? You were promoted by demonstrating that you had a proper understanding of the presented materials on a sliding scale of grades A, B, and C. Now compare what happens in the marketplace:

In an ideal scenario, "A" workers are promoted to jobs/opportunities of greater pay and responsibility

13

before "B" and "C" workers. Additionally, "B" workers should be promoted before "C" workers.

As you might imagine, "D" and "F" workers will only hold jobs with limited responsibility and lower pay. Also, realize that while in school, "D" and "F" students are typically held back in their current grades to relearn the materials.

In another illustration, once students graduate from high school and desire to enter college, grade point averages are used, in part, to determine who is accepted into specific colleges/universities. With the student's academic track record, schools of higher learning predict how productive the student will be within their campus environment. Are you beginning to see a pattern?

> **Key Principle: Grades are an important evaluation tool for prioritizing who receives opportunity. Ideally you want to be at the front of the opportunity line by being an "A" or "B" student in school.**

Recess

If you were like me, recess was the part of the school day that you really looked forward to. Do you believe that there was a marketplace application in going out to play with your friends? The answer, perhaps to your surprise, is a resounding yes.

Recess helped you hone invaluable social skills. Your ability to negotiate who took turns on the swing and who led in selecting the next game to play were important skills that translate into value in the marketplace.

An individual who has superior technical skills but poor people skills will have a difficult time in the marketplace because successful interactions with others are required to be productive in everyday life.

Recess was primarily a self-taught course where you should have learned leadership and conflict resolution skills. If unchecked, the playground bullies and habitual tattletales will, as adults, encounter problems climbing the ladder of success due to their inept social skills. Therefore, the "free time" associated with recess should have been leveraged to develop the interpersonal skills that are highly sought after in the marketplace.

> **Key Principle: A primary component to being productive is an individual's ability to get along with others.**

Establishing Self Worth and Contingent Destiny

The concepts I have presented to you are true and should be taken to heart; however, I realize that there are far too many kids out there who incorrectly believe that they are losers and feel as though they always will be. Sometimes this negative image of self is derived from a lack of confidence. Often this incorrect assessment comes from the cruelty of the world we live in.

From my own personal experience, I was excited by the prospect of obtaining an education because I felt it would help prepare me for the great things I would accomplish in life. The investment that I was making in my education was worthwhile because I had a positive self-image of who I was and who I would ultimately become along with supportive parents.

If you do not have a positive self-image or a clear positive vision of who you will become in the future, I challenge you to take a leap of faith by taking your education seriously. As you make a positive investment in yourself, you will slowly begin to see a positive return. As you reap the reward of getting A's and B's on your tests, you will start feeling better about yourself and your prospects. However, the worst thing you can do is to believe that your positive actions won't yield a bright future. This attitude will lead you to neglect the God-given talent that you have within you. In turn, you will miss out on experiencing the joy associated with being a producer.

Success is in reach for us all even though some people start out in more difficult environments than others. The good news is that our actions greatly impact our ultimate success.

Key Principle: Your destiny is contingent upon what actions you take today. So, make the most out of your life by taking your education seriously!

The Anti-Education Agenda

My hope is that you now have a firm understanding of why doing well in school is important. However, some of you may be thinking that you'll make your millions as the next pop icon.

Today we are flooded with images of pop icons racking in millions of dollars every year doing everything from musical performances to promoting products. Better yet, some people are making lots of money simply by being a celebrity personality who angles for media attention through reality shows, blogs, and the like. It seems fair to assume that the majority of these people were not straight A students in school, yet, they appear to be financially wealthy. One would assume doing well in school is not the only path to financial success, right?

The honest answer is yes. The key component of the marketplace is supplying consumer demand. While the educational system's goal is to develop you into a productive person, school is not the only place where you can receive an education. Many elite entertainers and athletes have spent lifetimes working hard at their crafts to get to where they are today by leveraging the valuable success skills I have already mentioned. Therefore, you can set yourself apart in the marketplace by having highly specialized skills.

The mistake that many young people make in believing they can simply brush off education to become the next pop icon is that they fail to realize true success requires hard work. When you skip school and neglect homework assignments, you allow laziness to destroy you from the inside out. The same disciplined attitude that compels you to come to class and study hard is the same state of mind needed to be successful in every area of your life. Lazy, undisciplined people succeed only in fooling themselves into believing that they can get serious when they choose to. Yet, their slothful habits will prove difficult to break and will keep them ineffective and nonproductive.

Fact: Becoming an educated person equips you with the skill set to prosper, even to multi-billionaire status throughout your life. Regardless of your career aspirations, doing well in school should always be a part of your success equation. It is foolish to have a 'sports vs. education' attitude. The correct attitude should lead you to be both the best student and athlete.

Entertainment superstardom is a status that few will ever achieve. It is also worth noting that far too many "stars" find themselves broke in the long run due to their poor decision-making abilities, which could have been developed if they would had taken their educations more seriously.

Key Principle: Procrastinators, the undisciplined, and people always looking for the easy way out will never maximize their full potential. Don't fool yourself by thinking there is an easy route to success.

Know Your History!

History

What is so important about studying old news? History—my favorite subject when I was growing up—is important because it provides clues about the present and the future.

For example, the United States began as an English colony. Consequently, the first waves of Europeans to this country were mostly of English descent.

When the colonists decided that America would be free of English rule, the forefathers drafted the Constitution and Bill of Rights, which were based on the English Magna Carta philosophy of citizens' rights.

Fast-forwarding through American history, the United States and England were allies in both world wars and are still close military allies today. You could conclude from your knowledge of history that if another country declares war on England, the United States would offer some form of assistance.

If you don't understand the historical ties between the U.S. and England, then it will be difficult to understand our relationship with the English today and even harder to predict how we might relate to them in the future.

As another example, economy activity can be classified in four categories: Depression, Boom, Recovery, and Recession.

A depression is an extreme decrease in economic growth. In this environment, even those with validated know-how will struggle to find livable wages. This economic condition occurred last in the late 1920s and early 1930s.

In an economic boom, the economy grows at a staggering rate. In this scenario, those with know-how earn premium wages. Even those without developed know-how may be able to secure decent wages for a limited period of time. The last economic boom, at the time of this publication, was in the late 1990s.

A recession means the economy has lost the growth seen in previous quarterly periods. Lastly, economic recovery simply means the economy is improving from a previous downturn.

Using historical data as our guide, we know that economic conditions tend to run in cycles. In fact, economic recoveries/booms typically last for approximately five years and recessions generally last for one year.

You could use this data to help manage your money and guide your investment decisions. For example, consider a scenario where the economy has been rapidly growing for the last five years. Based on your knowledge of economic history, you know that the end of this boom period is likely to come to an end soon. Therefore, you decide to start saving more money to increase your emergency funds, and you begin taking additional training courses to increase your know-how in preparation for a downturn. As a result, when the next recession hits, you will be in a better position to ride out the economic storm as opposed to someone who had no understanding of the historical nature of our economic cycles and, thus, enters a recession unprepared.

To further illustrate the marketplace application of my example above, consider the investment strategy utilized by Warren Buffett, CEO of Berkshire Hathaway and one of the richest men in the world. When looming recessions sharply drive down stock market values, Mr. Buffett buys large shares of companies while other people sell at a loss in a panicked state. Based on his knowledge of historical data, Mr. Buffett takes a calculated risk that stocks, on average, will typically rebound sharply as the economy improves. As a result, Mr. Buffett has made additional billions of dollars following the 2000 and 2009 recession periods. Importantly, since history tends to repeat itself, educated people anticipate and profit from predictable reoccurring events.

A person who understands history can approach a situation with, at the very least, an educated assumption of an anticipated future outcome. People who understand history realize that events don't just happen randomly; they are most often the end result of a series of past events/decisions. Therefore, the history topics you are studying in school today are giving you a foundation based on past events that influence current and future outcomes.

Those who don't understand history walk through life blindly. They are most often unable to accurately predict future outcomes because they lack the background facts necessary for making an educated assumption. In turn, their lack of knowledge negatively impacts all aspects of their life.

Subject point: History helps you understand current events and successfully predict future outcomes.

Address Your Class!

English/Language Arts

What's the big deal about studying English, especially if it is your native language? English, like all the other subjects you study in school, is highly important to your success. The primary purpose for studying English is to master the art of communicating with others.

Take a minute to think about the importance of communication. Consider the various ways in which we communicate today: telephone (verbal and text messaging), e-mail, letters, video, blogs, tweets, newspapers, face to face, gestures, signs, etc.

A society that does not communicate is a society that will not thrive. Communication is used to transfer information from one person to another so that individuals may take necessary action.

For example, consider a newborn baby. As we all know, babies learn over a period of time how to talk. When a baby is hungry or needs his diaper changed, he cries to get the attention of a caretaker who can help him. As this example illustrates, even babies know that communication is an essential survival technique.

Key Principle: Enhanced communication skills increase your chance of survival. Poor communication skills decrease your chance of survival.

Below I have segmented the subject of language arts into three categories: writing, reading, and speaking.

Writing

Written communication dates beyond ancient Egyptian and Greek civilizations. The major learning objective of written communication is to understand how to effectively put your thoughts on paper. The essential component of becoming a good writer is mastery of proper grammar, which includes the ability to formulate a proper sentence. Proper grammar and sentence structure allows your readers to understand the message you are conveying.

Today, texting has become a popular form of written communication. The frequent use of abbreviations and symbols, however, is not sufficient practice to master the art of writing.

In the marketplace, you will need to know how to formally communicate with investors, employees, clients, and/or other professionals. Formal written communication becomes a permanent record of a person's ability to effectively communicate. An inability to write effectively will cause others to question your know-how and will cause confusion and delays in business operations. As a result, you will be deemed as unreliable and your perceived value in the marketplace will drop tremendously because, as stated earlier, poor communication skills equal diminished chances of survival.

Reading

Reading and writing go closely together. To grasp the full importance of reading, take a moment to envision yourself in a foreign country. Imagine all the signs and postings that you wouldn't be able to understand. As a further example, go to a website in which the company offers a foreign language version. You will quickly notice that with the exception of familiar images, you will be clueless on how to navigate through the site.

In class, you read many American and English classics, such as TO KILL A MOCKINGBIRD and JULIUS CAESAR. But what do these works of the past have to do with modern times?

1. Reading books allow you to personally experience the true power of writing. Through the author's detailed development of the storyline and characters, they cleverly allow you to become an eyewitness to events that they are depicting on paper. Simply put, good authors allow your imagination to travel back in time or to a different place in order to relate to that particular setting. The books you read in class give you a vivid historical perspective of the attitudes of the past, which gives you a better understanding of present day motives and conditions.

2. Analyzing what you read develops your reading comprehension and critical thinking skills. After reading a literary work, you are often asked to review and discuss what happened within the

story. A person who goes through life unable to fully understand what they have read and how to make critical decisions based on that information is at an extreme disadvantage in the marketplace compared to someone who has mastered these skills. The vast majority of business arrangements require both parties to sign a written contract, confirming that they have read and understand the terms of the agreement. Without developing these skills, you will frequently be cheated, conned, and misled. This is why many scams are successfully targeted at undereducated and elderly communities. The scammers know that they will find people with underdeveloped or deteriorating comprehension and critical thinking skills to take advantage of.

Key Principle: Reading comprehension and critical thinking skills must be mastered to avoid being ripped off.

Speaking

Your speaking ability is directly tied to your reading and writing abilities. If you are a poor reader, then it is highly probable that you are also a poor writer and speaker. Reading affects your vocabulary, which in turns affects how well you speak. You often will find that people write the way they talk. Therefore, a person who uses a lot of slang when they speak will frequently use a lot of slang in their writing.

Speaking is the ultimate form of communication because it involves one-on-one personal contact. Regardless of what applied skills you possess, an inability to speak well in the marketplace will cost you opportunity.

Take advantage of opportunities to present in front of your classmates and hone your skill to articulate discussion points in class. These skills will pay huge dividends in the marketplace.

A note on slang talk: Slang talk amongst your peer group is a form of social identification. Taken in the proper context, speaking in slang is a normal part of maturing. However, frequently relying on slang terminology can negatively impact your perceived value in the marketplace. Recall that at the end of your educational pursuits you will be exchanging your know-how for money. Now ask yourself, who will be paying for your know-how? Your friends, investors, employers, or businesses/individuals? You answered correctly if you realized that more than likely your friends won't be cutting you a check to support your lifestyle. You must recognize that investors, employers, and businesses/individuals overwhelmingly frown on the use of slang. Therefore, slang is ultimately a counterproductive form of communication if you are aiming to be a producer outside your peer group.

Foreign Languages

Studying a foreign language is becoming increasingly important in the evolving global marketplace. In the past, studying a foreign language may have been viewed as simply an added bonus to formal education. Yet, with the wide use of the Internet, emerging markets, and increasing trade agreements, we must now look at learning multiple foreign languages as a means of increasing our recognized value in the marketplace.

Similar to learning and studying English, mastering a foreign language consists of being able to read, write, and speak the language in question. Just as we read American and English classics to gain an understanding of the attitudes and beliefs of American culture, you must also immerse yourself in the culture of the language you are studying through learning about the country's history, analyzing their political and family structures, and sampling traditional foods. By learning the culture as well as the language you will be better equipped to survive and prosper in the country in question.

You may be thinking I'm an American; why do I need to learn another language when many people around the world want to come here to live and learn English?

First, the fact that foreigners want to move to the United States equals opportunity in the marketplace for multilingual professionals. Take some time to do a job search, and you will discover that many American employers are paying a premium for workers who are fluent in their customers' native languages, i.e. Spanish.

Additionally, in a global economy, we can no longer assume that the vast majority of opportunities will reside in the United States. As we speak, a small trend of Americans moving out of the country as a means to prosper has already emerged. An ethnocentric view of not wanting to learn a foreign language will only limit your opportunities.

> **Subject point: Learning foreign languages allows you to effectively communicate with a greater number of people which increases your ability to seize opportunity in the global marketplace.**

Create Something!

Art

Art classes help to balance the skill sets you learn in other subject matters. Most of the subjects you study in school are grounded in absolutes, i.e. 1+1 = 2. However, the field of art is mostly concentrated in the abstract, characterized by loose rules and associations. In other words, art is all about creativity.

Over the years, I have always been amazed by what has been classified as a 'work of art.' Something that may look terrible to you could indeed be labeled a masterpiece by others and sold for millions of dollars because of a prospective buyer's appreciation for the artist's personal expression.

Consider the following marketplace applications related to the art field:

1. Art classes teach you that it is okay to be creative. Doing the same thing the same way all the time does not create new value. Your ability to produce results through your creativity will be highly treasured in the marketplace. Recall how the founders of Facebook, Groupon, and Google were able to translate their innovations into multi-billion dollar fortunes.

2. Art classes teach you courage. When you step out on a limb and exercise your creativity, it is only natural that you will

experience some form of anxiety resulting from producing something that may not be conventional. Your willingness to take this risk and defend your work against critics are key skill sets to develop.

3. Art also strengthens your communication skills. Visual art can be viewed as a non-verbal way of expressing a belief, detailing a period of time, or depicting the world around us.

Creativity is a key component of America's prosperity. Increasing the innovative solutions we bring to existing problems only strengthens our position as a world leader. Your ability to creatively, yet, efficiently address situations should result in premium earnings in the marketplace.

Subject point: Art helps you develop the creative skills most often necessary to bring new innovations (value) to the marketplace.

Be a Problem Solver!

Math

Throughout time, civilizations have used math to conduct business, erect structures, and function day to day. Math is considered a universal language since mathematic equations like 2+2 = 4 are the same all around the world.

The field of math, although not typically a favorite amongst students, teaches very important lessons that can be tied to the marketplace.

Math is rooted in absolutes and relationships. For example: 1+1 = 2; therefore, 2+1 = 3. As this example illustrates, once you have successfully reached a conclusion on a particular truth, then you can expand upon those facts to discover other truths.

Math teaches us how to be better linear thinkers. The basic component of linear thinking is applying an if/then scenario to what you are analyzing. For example, "if" you do not go to school, "then" you will not be promoted to the next grade. Or, "if" you study hard for a test, "then" you will increase your chances of receiving a good grade.

Although these examples may seem like plain common sense, mastering this method of thinking will help you become a stronger producer. Mathematical thinking helps us identify associations that maximize production and, thus, aids us in avoiding activities that minimize production or waste time.

Here is a brief analysis of three of the major math topics you study in school and how they relate to the marketplace:

Arithmetic

$1 + 1 = 2$

Arithmetic is the very basic but most often used form of math. Earlier in life you should have recognized that you need to know how to add, subtract, multiply, and divide to be functional. Our daily interaction with one another involves basic arithmetic whether you go to the mall to buy clothes with cash, or calculate how much money you will make at a job paying $7.00 per hour during a 15-hour work week. People with poor arithmetic skills will have difficulty surviving in the marketplace because either their inferior skills will inhibit them from becoming producers or they will be cheated out of the money they have earned.

Algebra

$3 + x = 11$

Algebra is a problem-solving tool that builds on basic arithmetic. In the equation above, we know that x is equal to 8 only because we first learned how to count. Using this same example, we also know that 11 minus 8 must equal 3. Through its analysis of relationships, algebra will help you reach conclusions with limited information.

It will sharpen your ability to identify associations of facts you already know to be true in order to lead you to an answer for the part of the scenario you are unsure of.

Geometry

$C = 2\pi r$

_{Equation for the perimeter of a circle}

The meaning of the word "geometry" can be translated as measurement of the earth. From this definition, geometry is mostly concentrated in the measurement of shapes such as circles and triangles. By gaining an understanding of objects, you can begin to develop if/then theories that can be proven.

Practical applications of geometry include any activity requiring you to build a structure, paint a room, sod a lawn, etc.

Geometry also helps develop your deductive reasoning skills, which are used to solve problems by taking something that is accepted as true and then applying it to all things that fit within the association. The following is an example of deductive reasoning:

- Johnny is a smart kid.

- Smart kids go to bed early and do their homework.

- Therefore, we can confidently conclude that Johnny goes to bed early and does his homework because he is a smart kid.

In short, mathematics helps us further develop the required marketplace skill set of being able to solve problems. Math teaches us to draw logical conclusions based on our understanding of known relationships.

Subject point: Math is incorporated into your everyday life and helps develop your problem-solving skills.

Discover Your Recipe for Success!

Science

The lessons learned in science are very closely tied to the skill sets learned from math. Through observation, scientists theorize on activities taking place in the world around us to arrive at certain universal truths or natural laws. For instance, Sir Isaac Newton was able to develop his famous law of gravity, explaining how the moon gravitates to earth by simply observing an apple fall. Through testing his theory, he eventually arrived at the following mathematical equation to explain how gravity affects objects:

$F = G m_1 m_2 / d^2$

Science's primary applications in the marketplace are to develop your critical thinking and research skills. The problem-solving technique of the scientific method has great value in the marketplace. The method consists of the following:

1. **Name a problem or question through personal observation**. As an example, we will ponder if increased formal education equals increased wages on average. As an observation, I will state that some people earn more money than others.

2. **Form an educated guess or hypothesis of what causes the problem to occur and make predications based upon the hypothesis.** In our example, I will hypothesize that people with higher degrees of education possess greater skills which positively affects how much money they make. I will also predict that someone who has a master's degree in a given field will, on average, earn more than a person with a bachelor's degree in the same field.

3. **Test the hypothesis through observing or analyzing data from a control group.** In our example, I would go to a university such as "State University" and research the average stated salaries of individuals who had received a bachelor's degree in business versus individuals who had received a master's degree in business. I might also do an online search of a particular employer with job openings within a business unit and analyze the stated salary range difference between the two levels of education.

4. **Check and interpret results.** Hypothetically, an analysis from State University revealed that their master's degreed individuals earned, on average, $20,000 more than individuals with just a

bachelor's degree. Also, an analysis of my online job opening search highlighted that in positions requiring at least 10 years of experience; bachelor's degreed individuals' salary ranges were 25% less than those with a master's degree. These two independent tests seem to suggest that increased formal education does equal more pay for individuals.

5. **Conclusion**. After I have eliminated any obvious errors in my testing, such as not ensuring that the master's and bachelor's graduates have spent the same amount of time in the workforce, then I could finally conclude that the more education I obtain, the more money I will earn, on average. This conclusion should influence me to pursue higher degrees of education—definitely beyond a high school diploma.

Key Principle: Individuals who can systematically gather data to reach a clearer assumption of the effects of their actions will be paid a premium in the marketplace.

The following is an analysis of two major fields of science and how they relate directly to the marketplace:

Biology

Biology is the study of life. It examines the interdependence of cells which come together to form organisms such as humans and animals as well as tiny microorganisms like bacteria and plankton.

Biologists have discovered that the human body is very complex. In fact, our bodies are made up of numerous systems: digestive, respiratory and circulatory, musculoskeletal, and nervous. All of these systems must function together in harmony for us to be healthy.

The marketplace value of studying biology is learning that life, in general, is made up of complex systems. For example, to enjoy the freedoms you have today, our country's judicial, political, defense, social, education, economic, and legislative systems must all function in harmony similar to our bodies.

Biology teaches us that all life interacts with various systems. It also helps give us the tools to break down what those systems are and how they interrelate. Importantly, a person who struggles to identify the structure and interrelationship of various systems in the marketplace will find it difficult to be productive.

Chemistry

Chemistry is the study of matter and its observed interaction with energy. Matter can be defined as anything that you can touch, see, hear, smell, and/or taste. All matter is made up of a combination of over 100 elements such as calcium (CA) and sodium (NA) which are represented on the periodic table you may have seen in class. It is noteworthy that each new combination of elements creates a new form of matter. In addition, energy can be defined as a source of usable power. What does all this translate to? The entire world around us involves some form of chemistry.

From a practical approach, the next time you drink a soda, take a moment to study the ingredients on the side of the can. Through a chemical reaction, all of the individual ingredients come together to deliver the taste that you love. Furthermore, that same drink you may enjoy, such as ginger ale, could also be used to remove a stain on your favorite shirt from the chemical reaction between the liquid and the fabric.

What does learning about a bunch of chemical reactions have to do with your life? Chemistry also helps us understand that everything has a composition. For instance, the range of subjects you study in school over a multitude of years compromises "formal education." Your attitude regarding these subjects, combined with your teachers' ability to convey their know-how, in a sense creates a reaction in the form of acquired knowledge that potential employers, investors, and businesses/individuals use to judge your skills.

An individual who understands the concept of composition will have an advantage in being creative (adding value). They will understand, for example, that they can experiment with various resources to develop more efficient ways of doing things. From a leadership perspective, they will also understand that "team chemistry," ensuring that each individual's skills complement the skill sets of other team members, is a key element to success. As with chemistry, the ability to identify and manage resources (matter) are both valuable marketplace skills.

> **Subject Point: Science helps you develop a thought process to arrive at a reasonable conclusion. In the marketplace, and life in general, we arrive at decision points with limited information.**

Develop Your Competitive Edge!

Sports

Sports are also a very important component to your overall learning. As I stated earlier, an athlete who is a star on the field, yet fails in the classroom, demonstrates that they have not gained a true understanding of the lessons that should be learned from sports. Let's consider the marketplace value you can acquire from playing organized sports:

Practice Influences Performance

All team sports require strategic planning and repetition. As an athlete, you go through drills to enhance your overall performance that are somewhat indirectly related to the sport you are playing. For example, football players spend significant time in the weight room building muscle that will ultimately help them perform better during a game.

While you are in the midst of this 'practice stage' you will typically sweat and tire as you execute the various drills. However, as you practice more and more you will undoubtedly hone your skills and your body will build up the required endurance to help you perform at your best.

Therefore, at the start of your first game, you should be prepared to compete successfully. As the game goes on, however, you will more than likely discover that some things that went well during practice do not always have the same outcome during the game. This difference could derive from underestimating your competition or overestimating how well you prepared. After the game, your team will assess what went right and what went wrong. Any corrections that need to be made can be addressed with a change of strategy or increased focus in an identified area of opportunity.

In relation to the real world, going to school is the practice field and the marketplace is the playing field. The subjects that you study in class are the drills that most often affect your ability to be successful in the marketplace. Your homework and other formal assignments can be viewed as the required blood, sweat, and tears that develop your potential and make you competitive. Tests and quizzes can be viewed as playing scrimmage games; they allow you to assess how well you have prepared yourself and highlight any adjustments that need to be made.

Teamwork Is Essential

The vast majority of sports involve reliance upon teammates. Think for a moment about the essence of team sports—individuals collectively utilizing their skills to achieve a common goal.

A sports team is like any organization. Roles, responsibilities, and goals must be defined; there is also high emphasis on coordinating each member's efforts. As a result, the communication skills that you develop in your language arts classes are essential to getting all team members on the same page.

Team leaders or captains typically emerge as you bring together people with different talents and skills. Leaders are looked upon to provide direction and necessary motivation to the team as needed.

Returning to our football analogy, consider all the different positions on a team and how each individual must do his assigned job for the unit to succeed. If a football team has a great offense but a lousy defense, then the imbalance of the team's skills will more than likely result in a loss. As another example, a linesman who fails to block an oncoming rusher will prevent the quarterback from getting the ball to an open wide receiver down field.

Another important aspect of team sports is again the concept of being present. When members of your team do not show up for practice, it is highly likely that the team will not gel together as one unit. This can lead to mistakes during games and a losing record.

You probably already see the real world application to the team sport concept. From a big picture perspective, we bring our individual skills into the marketplace as Americans for the collective good of the American economy (our team). On your job you will be assigned a certain number of tasks that all support your company's effort to make a profit and/or reach its goals. Additionally, as you hone your leadership skills on the playing field or in the classroom, your value in the marketplace will rise due to your ability to lead people toward organizational success.

Again, if you fail to show up on a consistent basis, then you bring no value to your team, company, or the economy, regardless of what your natural abilities may be.

Making the cut

Team sports also drive home the competitive nature of the marketplace. Consider how teams have a roster of starters and reservists. How does a team determine who will start and who does not?

To be a starter it is assumed that a particular person performs best at that position compared to all the available members on the team. This skill superiority is typically determined through the coaching staff's assessment of how individuals perform during tryouts and in practice as well as an assessment of how they play in games.

Reservists are also important members of the team because they fill in when their teammates get tired or are injured. Occasionally, reservists are able to move into the starting lineup when they showcase superior mastery of skills.

The point I want you to grasp here is the correlation between opportunities emerging from proving yourself. Sports teams typically hold tryouts each year to determine who will make the team. People who were on the team last year have an advantage over others trying to make the team because the coaching staff already has a feel for their abilities. Also, last year's players already have an understanding of the team's dynamics.

Accordingly, starters will also come in with an inherent advantage over reservists when coaches are determining who will start the new season.

Importantly, people who don't make the team won't have any opportunity to score a touchdown because they are simply not part of the team. Reservists may or may not get to play in a big game unless someone gets hurt. Yet, the starters have the opportunity to play every game, so they have the opportunity to impress college scouts and receive college scholarships. Following this scenario, I hope you can see that individuals who fail to prepare themselves prior to the tryouts now face an uphill battle becoming a starter or joining the team at all in the future.

The marketplace application is simple: you must properly prepare yourself if you expect to capitalize on opportunity. In life, your skills will always be compared to others; therefore, preparation is essential.

> **Key Principle: Strong performance leads to increased exposure which yields increased pay and, consequently, new lucrative opportunities. Poor performance most often limits opportunities and repositions you behind other people, forcing you, in effect, to wait for another chance to prove yourself.**

Education is your method of preparation. Individuals with poor educational foundations perform worse, in general, than individuals with strong educational foundations. In turn, those unprepared are placed on paths that make it difficult to score touchdowns (build wealth) throughout their lives.

Conclusion

Let's take a moment to reflect on the key principles and subject points shared throughout this book.

- Education is a very important area of your life, and you must learn to voluntarily choose it over other available activities if you want to succeed.

- You are in school to learn how to be a producer, which translates into being a person who adds tangible value to the world around you.

- The end result of your formal education is not a job. Your education is an important survival toolkit that will help you produce various sources of income, regardless of a particular economic environment.

- School is a practice run for what you will face as an adult; the sooner you understand and master this concept, the better off you will be later in life.

- The only way that you can effectively learn is to be consistently present.

- Grades are an important evaluation tool for prioritizing who receives opportunity. Ideally, you want to be at the front of the opportunity line by being an "A" or "B" student in school.

- A primary component to being productive is an individual's ability to get along with others.

- Your destiny is contingent upon what actions you take today.

- Procrastinators, the undisciplined, and people always looking for the easy way out will never maximize their full potential. Don't fool yourself by thinking there is an easy route to success.

- History helps you understand current events and successfully predict future outcomes.

- Enhanced communication skills increase your chance of survival. Poor communication skills decrease your chance of survival.

- Reading comprehension and critical thinking skills must be mastered to avoid being ripped off.

- Language arts help you master the art of communication, which will increase your value in the marketplace.

- Learning foreign languages allows you to effectively communicate with a greater number of people which increases your ability to seize opportunity in the global marketplace.

- Art helps you develop the creative skills most often necessary to bring new innovations (value) to the marketplace.

- Math is incorporated into your everyday life and helps you develop problem-solving skills.

- Science helps you develop a thought process to arrive at a reasonable conclusion. In the marketplace and life in general, we arrive at decision points with limited information.

- Individuals who can systematically gather data to reach a clearer assumption of the effects of their actions will be paid a premium in the marketplace.

- Strong performance leads to increased exposure which yields increased pay and, consequently, new lucrative opportunities. Poor performance most often limits opportunities and repositions you behind other people, forcing you, in effect, to wait for another chance to prove yourself.

In summary, your education is your opportunity to prepare yourself for the ultimate positive impact you will have on the world. The subject matters you are exposed to in school will not only help you solve tomorrow's problems, but will also give you the skill set to systematically make better life decisions today.

The world needs your best, and you deserve the joy associated with reaching your full potential. Therefore, view your education as an opportunity to become your best rather than a government requirement. Enjoy the journey to your zenith!

About the Author

C.B. Schooler is one who has always been excited by the possibilities of life. In 2007, he started Zenith Publishing to produce uplifting material to inspire people to become the best that they can be. His first book, "More Than Entertainers: An Inspirational Black Career Guide," won a national NAACP Image Award for outstanding teen literary work in 2008. He is also the creator of the nationally-recognized financial literacy web site, ChoiceNerd.com. In 2010, he was 1 of 28 personalities/celebrities featured during AT&T's Movers & Shakers national campaign.

He has stood before diverse audiences across the country speaking on topics such as education, community empowerment, and financial literacy.

C.B. Schooler holds a MBA degree from Xavier University in Cincinnati, Ohio, and has nearly 15 years of Fortune 500 corporate experience. Lastly, he recently founded the Center for Education Awareness to further address education attainment/achievement issues across the country.

Follow the author on Twitter @theSchooler and www.understandingschool.com

About the Illustrator

Gary Young is a native of Dayton, Ohio. He is a graduate of Roosevelt High School and Kent State University, where he studied Graphic Design and Illustration.

"As a kid, I had a big interest in comics and animation. The chapter illustrations I created for this book take me back to the educational drawings I grew up with, and were fun to do!"

Gary Young is the creator of the comic strip Cashews and is also a NAACP Image Award-winning illustrator for his work on "More Than Entertainers."

He currently works in the design field in New York City where he and his wife reside.